AMAZON NOVA
The Power Play in the AI Arena

Everything You Need to Know – From Generative Models to Artificial Intelligence Hardware and Beyond

J. Andy Peters

Copyright ©J. Andy Peters, *2024*.

All rights reserved. No part of this publication may be reproduced, distributed, or transmitted in any form or by any means, including photocopying, recording, or other electronic or mechanical methods, without the prior written permission of the publisher, except in the case of brief quotations embodied in critical reviews and certain other noncommercial uses permitted by copyright law.

Table of Contents

Introduction 3
Chapter 1: Amazon's Strategic Vision in AI 8
Chapter 2: Unveiling Amazon Nova 18
Chapter 3: Strategic Partnerships and Collaborations 29
Chapter 4: Integrating AI Across Amazon's Operations 36
Chapter 5: Innovative Shopping Experiences 47
Chapter 6: Amazon's Foray into AI Hardware 59
Chapter 7: Market Perception and Stock Performance 70
Chapter 8: Comparative Analysis with Other AI Leaders 80
Chapter 9: Real-World Impact and Future Implications 95
Chapter 10: Challenges and Opportunities Ahead 110
Chapter 11: Ethical Considerations and Responsible AI 118
Conclusion 123

Introduction

In recent years, the landscape of technology has undergone a seismic shift, propelled by the rapid advancements in artificial intelligence. What was once the realm of science fiction has now become an integral part of our daily lives, reshaping industries from healthcare to finance, and transforming the way businesses operate. This AI revolution is not merely about the introduction of new tools or systems; it's about a fundamental change in how we approach problem-solving, decision-making, and innovation. As machines become increasingly adept at tasks that once required human intelligence, the potential for growth and efficiency in various sectors has expanded exponentially.

Amidst this transformative wave, Amazon has emerged as a formidable player, strategically positioning itself at the forefront of the AI movement. Traditionally known for its dominance in e-commerce and cloud computing, Amazon has been quietly building the foundations of what is now a comprehensive artificial intelligence empire. The company's latest venture, Amazon Nova, signifies a bold leap into the AI arena, aiming to compete directly with established entities like OpenAI's ChatGPT. This strategic pivot is not just about keeping pace with the evolving technological landscape but about setting new standards and pushing the boundaries of what AI can achieve.

Amazon's commitment to AI is multifaceted, encompassing everything from developing sophisticated generative models to creating cutting-edge AI hardware. By launching a suite of models under the Nova brand, Amazon is addressing a wide array of applications, each tailored to meet specific needs. Whether it's enhancing customer service with more intuitive chatbots, optimizing logistics through advanced predictive models, or empowering sellers with automated tools, Amazon is leveraging AI to streamline operations and enhance user experiences across its vast ecosystem. This comprehensive approach underscores Amazon's vision of integrating AI into every facet of its business, ensuring that the company remains a dominant force in the tech industry.

The purpose of this book is to provide an in-depth exploration of Amazon's strategic foray into artificial intelligence. Readers will gain a thorough understanding of how Amazon Nova is revolutionizing the AI landscape, the innovative partnerships that are driving these advancements, and the tangible impacts of AI integration on Amazon's operations and market position. By delving into the specifics of Amazon's AI initiatives, this book aims to shed light on the company's methods, motivations, and the broader implications of its AI strategies.

Understanding Amazon's AI initiatives is crucial for several reasons. Firstly, Amazon's influence extends far beyond its core businesses, affecting various sectors through its extensive cloud services, marketplace, and consumer products. The company's advancements in AI have the potential to set industry standards and influence the direction of technological development globally. Secondly, as AI continues to evolve, the strategies employed by leading companies like Amazon offer valuable insights into the future of work, automation, and the ethical considerations that come with such powerful technologies. Finally, for investors, entrepreneurs, and tech enthusiasts, comprehending Amazon's AI trajectory provides a window into the next generation of innovation and the opportunities it presents.

Throughout this book, readers will embark on a journey that uncovers the layers of Amazon's AI strategy. From the inception of Amazon Nova and its various iterations to the intricate collaborations with other AI pioneers, each chapter will unravel the complexities and successes that define Amazon's approach to artificial intelligence. The narrative will also examine the practical applications of AI within Amazon's operations, showcasing how the company leverages technology to enhance efficiency, reduce costs, and improve customer satisfaction. Additionally, the book will explore Amazon's venture into AI hardware, highlighting its efforts to challenge industry giants like Nvidia and establish a foothold in the competitive AI hardware market.

By the end of this exploration, readers will not only understand the mechanics behind Amazon's AI advancements but also appreciate the broader significance of these developments in shaping the future of technology and business. This comprehensive analysis aims to equip readers with the knowledge to navigate the rapidly changing AI landscape, inspired by one of the most influential companies driving this transformation.

Chapter 1: Amazon's Strategic Vision in AI

In the fiercely competitive realm of artificial intelligence, Amazon stands out not just as a participant but as a formidable contender shaping the future of the industry. The AI landscape is populated by several key players, each bringing unique strengths and innovations to the table. Among the most prominent competitors are OpenAI, with its widely recognized ChatGPT, Google through its DeepMind and TensorFlow initiatives, Microsoft leveraging its extensive cloud services in partnership with OpenAI, and Nvidia, renowned for its powerful GPU technologies that fuel many AI applications. Additionally, emerging firms like Anthropic are making significant strides, offering advanced AI models that challenge the status quo and push the boundaries of what artificial intelligence can achieve.

Despite the presence of these established giants, Amazon carves out a distinctive position in the AI arena, leveraging its vast and multifaceted ecosystem to gain a competitive edge. One of Amazon's most significant advantages lies in its unparalleled cloud computing infrastructure, Amazon Web Services (AWS). AWS is not only a backbone for countless businesses worldwide but also a critical enabler for Amazon's own AI initiatives. By hosting its AI models on AWS, Amazon ensures scalability, reliability, and accessibility, allowing it to deploy sophisticated AI solutions efficiently and effectively.

Moreover, Amazon's deep integration of AI across its diverse range of services provides it with a unique advantage. Unlike competitors who may focus primarily on specific aspects of AI, Amazon seamlessly incorporates artificial intelligence into its e-commerce platform, logistics, customer service, and even entertainment through Amazon Prime Video. This holistic approach means that AI is not just a standalone feature but a core component that enhances every facet of Amazon's operations, driving efficiency and creating superior customer experiences.

Another cornerstone of Amazon's competitive advantage is its strategic partnerships, notably with Anthropic. By collaborating closely with leading AI firms, Amazon not only gains access to cutting-edge technologies but also fosters an environment of innovation and shared expertise. This symbiotic relationship allows Amazon to stay at the forefront of AI advancements, ensuring that its offerings remain competitive and continuously evolving to meet market demands.

Furthermore, Amazon's commitment to developing its own AI hardware sets it apart from many of its competitors. The company's investment in creating proprietary AI chips, such as the Tranium, and building supercomputers like the Ultra Cluster underscores its dedication to controlling and optimizing the hardware that powers its AI models. This vertical integration not only reduces dependency on external suppliers like Nvidia but also allows Amazon to tailor its hardware precisely to the needs of its AI applications, enhancing performance and cost-effectiveness.

Amazon's extensive data resources also play a pivotal role in its AI dominance. With access to vast amounts of consumer data through its e-commerce platform, AWS, and other services, Amazon can train its AI models with unprecedented depth and accuracy. This data-driven approach ensures that Amazon's AI solutions are not only powerful but also highly relevant and personalized, delivering value that resonates with users on a granular level.

In essence, while Amazon navigates a competitive landscape crowded with innovative minds and cutting-edge technologies, its unique blend of robust infrastructure, integrated AI applications, strategic partnerships, proprietary hardware development, and vast data resources positions it as a leader poised to redefine the boundaries of artificial intelligence. By capitalizing on these strengths, Amazon not only competes with the best in the industry but also sets new benchmarks for what AI can achieve in transforming businesses and enhancing everyday life.

Amazon's journey into the realm of artificial intelligence has been both strategic and visionary, culminating in the creation of Amazon Nova. The inception of Nova was not a spontaneous decision but rather the result of years of observation, innovation, and a deep understanding of the technological landscape. Recognizing the transformative potential of AI, Amazon sought to harness its capabilities to enhance every facet of its vast operations and maintain its competitive edge in an increasingly digital world.

The inspiration behind launching Nova stemmed from Amazon's relentless pursuit of efficiency and excellence. As the company expanded its footprint across various industries—from e-commerce and cloud computing to entertainment and logistics—it became evident that integrating advanced AI models could unlock unprecedented levels of performance and customer satisfaction. The success of conversational AI platforms like OpenAI's ChatGPT highlighted the immense possibilities that generative models offered, not just in enhancing user interactions but also in driving innovation across business processes. Amazon saw an opportunity to leverage similar technologies to streamline its operations, improve customer experiences, and offer new, intelligent services to its vast user base.

The objectives of Amazon Nova were clear and ambitious. At its core, Nova was designed to be a versatile suite of AI models capable of addressing a wide range of applications within and beyond Amazon's ecosystem. By developing multiple versions—Nova Micro, Nova Light, Nova Pro, Nova Premiere, Nova Canvas, and Nova Real—Amazon aimed to provide tailored solutions that could meet diverse needs, from simple text processing to complex image and video generation. This modular approach ensured that businesses of all sizes and across different sectors could find a Nova model that best suited their specific requirements, thereby democratizing access to cutting-edge AI technology.

Moreover, Amazon intended Nova to serve as a cornerstone for its broader AI strategy, which emphasizes scalability, reliability, and integration. By embedding Nova into its existing infrastructure, particularly Amazon Web Services (AWS), the company could offer these powerful AI tools to a global audience, enhancing the value proposition of AWS and solidifying Amazon's position as a leader in cloud-based AI solutions. This alignment with AWS not only provided Nova with the necessary computational power and scalability but also facilitated seamless integration with other Amazon services, creating a cohesive and intelligent ecosystem.

Amazon Nova's launch was also a strategic move to counter the growing competition in the AI space. With major players like Google, Microsoft, and Nvidia advancing rapidly, Amazon needed to establish its own formidable presence to ensure it remained at the forefront of technological innovation. By developing proprietary AI models and investing in AI hardware, Amazon aimed to reduce its reliance on external providers and gain greater control over its AI capabilities. This vertical integration was crucial for maintaining a competitive advantage, allowing Amazon to tailor its AI solutions more precisely to its operational needs and customer demands.

Aligning with Amazon's long-term goals, Nova represents a significant step towards creating a more intelligent and autonomous organization. The integration of AI across various departments—from customer service and logistics to product recommendations and entertainment—ensures that Amazon can continuously innovate and improve its services. By automating routine tasks, optimizing supply chains, and providing personalized experiences, Nova helps Amazon enhance operational efficiency and deliver superior value to its customers. This not only drives customer loyalty and satisfaction but also positions Amazon to capitalize on emerging opportunities in the AI-driven future.

Furthermore, Nova's development underscores Amazon's commitment to ethical and responsible AI usage. As AI technologies become more pervasive, concerns around bias, privacy, and security grow. Amazon has taken proactive measures to ensure that its AI models are designed and deployed with these considerations in mind, striving to create fair, transparent, and secure AI solutions. This responsible approach not only builds trust with customers and partners but also sets a benchmark for the industry, reinforcing Amazon's reputation as a trustworthy and forward-thinking technology leader.

In essence, the genesis of Amazon Nova is a testament to Amazon's strategic foresight and unwavering dedication to innovation. By launching Nova, Amazon not only addresses immediate business needs but also lays the groundwork for sustained growth and leadership in the AI landscape. Nova embodies Amazon's vision of a future where artificial intelligence seamlessly integrates with every aspect of business and daily life, driving progress and creating new possibilities for both the company and its global community of customers.

Chapter 2: Unveiling Amazon Nova

Amazon Nova represents a groundbreaking advancement in the field of artificial intelligence, embodying Amazon's ambitious vision to redefine the capabilities and applications of AI across various industries. At its core, Nova is a comprehensive suite of foundation models meticulously designed to cater to a diverse range of needs, both within Amazon's vast ecosystem and beyond. This suite is not a single monolithic model but a collection of specialized versions, each tailored to address specific challenges and optimize different aspects of AI functionality.

The foundation of Amazon Nova lies in its modular architecture, which includes distinct versions such as Nova Micro, Nova Light, Nova Pro, Nova Premiere, Nova Canvas, and Nova Real. Each variant is engineered with unique capabilities to serve different purposes. Nova Micro, for instance, is a text-only model that offers cost-effective and low-latency solutions for straightforward text processing tasks. Moving up the spectrum, Nova Light introduces multimodal capabilities, allowing it to handle not just text but also images and videos with remarkable speed and efficiency. This makes it an ideal choice for applications that require quick processing of diverse data types without compromising on performance.

Nova Pro strikes a balance between accuracy, speed, and cost, making it a versatile option for a wide array of tasks that demand reliable performance without exorbitant expenses. For more complex and demanding applications, Nova Premiere steps in, offering advanced reasoning capabilities that enable it to tackle intricate problems and perform sophisticated analyses. This version is particularly suited for scenarios that require deep understanding and nuanced responses, setting it apart from more basic models.

In addition to these, Nova Canvas and Nova Real expand the suite's functionality into the realms of image and video generation. Nova Canvas excels in creating high-quality images based on textual descriptions, while Nova Real pushes the boundaries further by generating realistic videos, opening up new possibilities for content creation, entertainment, and interactive experiences. These tools not only enhance the creative potential of users but also provide businesses with powerful assets to engage their audiences in innovative ways.

What truly distinguishes Amazon Nova from existing AI models is its strategic integration with Amazon's extensive infrastructure and its focus on scalability and versatility. Unlike many AI models that operate in isolation, Nova is deeply embedded within Amazon Web Services (AWS), leveraging the cloud giant's robust and scalable infrastructure to deliver seamless performance across a global network. This integration ensures that Nova can handle large-scale deployments efficiently, making it accessible to a wide range of users from startups to multinational corporations.

Furthermore, Amazon Nova's collaboration with Anthropic, a leading AI research company, adds another layer of differentiation. This partnership allows Amazon to incorporate cutting-edge advancements and insights from Anthropic into the Nova suite, enhancing its capabilities and keeping it at the forefront of AI innovation. By combining Amazon's vast resources and infrastructure with Anthropic's specialized expertise, Nova is positioned to deliver superior performance and stay ahead of the competition in an ever-evolving AI landscape.

Another key differentiator is Amazon's commitment to affordability and accessibility. By offering multiple versions of Nova tailored to different use cases and budget constraints, Amazon ensures that businesses of all sizes can harness the power of advanced AI without prohibitive costs. This democratization of AI technology not only broadens the potential user base but also fosters innovation by enabling more companies to integrate AI into their operations and products.

Moreover, the versatility of Amazon Nova extends beyond its technical specifications. The suite is designed to be user-friendly, with intuitive interfaces and comprehensive support, allowing users to easily deploy and manage AI applications without requiring deep technical expertise. This focus on ease of use empowers a broader audience to leverage AI, from developers and data scientists to marketers and customer service teams, enhancing productivity and driving value across the board.

In essence, Amazon Nova is more than just a collection of AI models; it is a strategic initiative that encapsulates Amazon's vision for the future of artificial intelligence. By offering a diverse range of tailored solutions, integrating seamlessly with a powerful cloud infrastructure, fostering strategic partnerships, and prioritizing affordability and accessibility, Nova sets itself apart from existing AI models. It embodies a holistic approach to AI development and deployment, ensuring that businesses and individuals alike can tap into the transformative potential of artificial intelligence to drive innovation, efficiency, and growth.

Amazon Nova stands as a testament to Amazon's dedication to advancing artificial intelligence, offering a diverse array of models tailored to meet specific needs across various applications. At the heart of the Nova suite is Nova Micro, a text-only model designed for efficiency and simplicity. This model excels in handling straightforward text processing tasks, providing users with a cost-effective solution that delivers quick and reliable results without the complexities of more advanced models. Its streamlined functionality makes it an ideal choice for businesses seeking to enhance their text-based operations without incurring significant expenses.

Building upon the foundation laid by Nova Micro, Nova Light introduces multimodal capabilities, seamlessly integrating text, images, and videos into a single, cohesive model. This versatility allows users to manage and process diverse types of data with ease, making Nova Light particularly valuable for applications that require a blend of visual and textual information. Whether it's analyzing multimedia content, generating comprehensive reports, or enhancing interactive user experiences, Nova Light offers the flexibility needed to address a wide range of business challenges efficiently.

For organizations seeking a balanced approach to AI, Nova Pro emerges as the optimal solution. This model strikes an impressive balance between accuracy, speed, and cost, making it suitable for a broad spectrum of tasks that demand reliable performance without breaking the bank. Nova Pro is engineered to handle more complex operations, providing enhanced precision and faster processing times compared to its predecessors. This makes it an excellent fit for businesses that require dependable AI capabilities to support their core functions while maintaining budgetary constraints.

Taking AI sophistication to the next level, Nova Premiere is designed for advanced reasoning and intricate problem-solving. This model is equipped to tackle complex scenarios that demand deep understanding and nuanced responses, setting it apart from more basic models. Nova Premiere's ability to engage in sophisticated analyses and deliver insightful outcomes makes it an invaluable tool for industries that rely on high-level decision-making and strategic planning. Its advanced capabilities ensure that businesses can leverage AI to address the most challenging aspects of their operations with confidence and precision.

Expanding the suite's functionality further, Nova Canvas and Nova Real focus on the realms of image and video generation. Nova Canvas specializes in creating high-quality images from textual descriptions, empowering users to generate visual content that aligns perfectly with their creative visions. This capability is particularly beneficial for marketing, advertising, and content creation, where compelling visuals are essential for engagement and communication. On the other hand, Nova Real pushes the boundaries of what's possible by generating realistic videos, opening up new avenues for interactive experiences, entertainment, and dynamic content delivery. Together, these models enhance the creative potential of users, providing powerful tools to produce engaging and visually stunning media.

The practical applications of Amazon Nova span across various sectors, each leveraging the suite's diverse capabilities to drive innovation and efficiency. In the realm of customer service, Nova's advanced chatbots streamline interactions, providing instant and accurate responses to customer inquiries, thereby enhancing satisfaction and reducing operational costs. Retail businesses utilize Nova Light and Nova Pro to optimize inventory management, predict demand more accurately, and personalize customer experiences through targeted recommendations. In the healthcare industry, Nova Premiere aids in complex data analysis and diagnostics, enabling medical professionals to make more informed decisions and improve patient outcomes.

Case studies further illustrate the profound impact of Nova on different industries. A leading e-commerce platform implemented Nova Micro to automate their customer support, resulting in a significant reduction in response times and a notable increase in customer satisfaction scores. Meanwhile, a major logistics company integrated Nova Light into their supply chain operations, enhancing their ability to forecast demand and manage inventory more effectively, which led to cost savings and improved delivery times. In the creative sector, a renowned advertising agency employed Nova Canvas to generate innovative visual content, allowing them to produce high-quality marketing materials swiftly and efficiently, thereby boosting their competitive edge in the market.

Through these implementations, Amazon Nova demonstrates its ability to adapt to the unique needs of various industries, providing tailored AI solutions that drive tangible benefits. Whether it's improving operational efficiency, enhancing customer experiences, or fostering innovation, the Nova suite equips businesses with the tools they need to thrive in an increasingly AI-driven world. By offering a range of models that cater to different requirements, Amazon ensures that Nova remains a versatile and indispensable asset for organizations seeking to harness the full potential of artificial intelligence.

Chapter 3: Strategic Partnerships and Collaborations

As Amazon's vision for artificial intelligence continued to evolve, forging closer connections with organizations at the forefront of cutting-edge research became a natural step. In seeking collaborators who could complement its ambition, Amazon found a valuable partner in Anthropic, a company focused on advancing AI models with remarkable depth of understanding and robustness. By deepening their ties, both sides gained more than just technological advantages. Amazon's extensive cloud infrastructure and global reach provided Anthropic with unparalleled resources to train and deploy its latest innovations, while Anthropic's research-driven ethos and willingness to push the boundaries of what AI could achieve infused Amazon's initiatives with fresh perspectives. This partnership was about more than simply merging tools or swapping services; it was an alliance born from a shared belief that the ultimate trajectory of AI should be guided by thoughtful research, ethical principles, and a commitment to building systems that benefit everyone. In collaborating, they not only pooled intellectual capital but also aligned their goals, intent on shaping a future where intelligent systems deliver meaningful value, address real-world challenges, and evolve responsibly. The synergy created through this partnership fortified Amazon's position in the competitive AI landscape and gave Anthropic the breadth and scale it needed to realize its most ambitious projects, ensuring that both parties would continue to thrive as they explored the next frontier of artificial intelligence.

Amazon's commitment to advancing artificial intelligence is not solely driven by in-house innovation; it is significantly bolstered by strategic collaborations that amplify its capabilities and accelerate progress. One of the most pivotal partnerships in this journey is with Anthropic, a company renowned for its cutting-edge AI research and development. This alliance exemplifies how collaborative efforts can lead to groundbreaking advancements and elevate the overall quality of AI technologies.

The partnership between Amazon and Anthropic is rooted in a shared vision of pushing the boundaries of what artificial intelligence can achieve. By pooling their respective strengths, both companies have embarked on joint projects that have yielded significant breakthroughs in AI model development and deployment. One such initiative involves the integration of Anthropic's sophisticated AI models with Amazon's robust cloud infrastructure provided by Amazon Web Services (AWS). This synergy allows for the training and scaling of complex AI models that neither company could efficiently develop independently.

A notable breakthrough from this collaboration is the enhancement of generative AI capabilities. Anthropic's expertise in creating models that understand and generate human-like text complements Amazon's extensive data resources and computational power. Together, they have developed more nuanced and contextually aware AI systems that can handle a wider array of tasks with greater accuracy and reliability. These advancements are not just incremental improvements; they represent a significant leap forward in the sophistication and applicability of AI technologies.

Beyond technical enhancements, the partnership has also fostered a culture of shared knowledge and continuous innovation. Regular joint workshops, research exchanges, and collaborative development sessions ensure that both teams stay at the forefront of AI advancements. This environment of mutual learning and support accelerates the pace of innovation, enabling both Amazon and Anthropic to respond swiftly to emerging challenges and opportunities in the AI landscape.

One of the standout projects emerging from this collaboration is the development of advanced natural language processing (NLP) models that are more adept at understanding context, intent, and nuance in human communication. These models are being integrated into Amazon Nova, enhancing its ability to provide more accurate and meaningful interactions across various applications, from customer service chatbots to sophisticated data analysis tools. The improved NLP capabilities allow Amazon to offer more personalized and efficient services, thereby elevating the user experience and driving greater customer satisfaction.

Moreover, the collaboration has extended into the realm of AI ethics and responsible AI deployment. Both Amazon and Anthropic recognize the importance of developing AI systems that are not only powerful but also fair, transparent, and accountable. Joint efforts in this area have led to the establishment of robust frameworks for ethical AI usage, ensuring that their technologies are developed and implemented in ways that prioritize user trust and societal well-being. This commitment to ethical AI practices sets a high standard for the industry and underscores the significance of responsible innovation.

The mutual benefits of this partnership are evident in the enhanced capabilities and expanded reach of both companies. For Amazon, collaborating with Anthropic means gaining access to some of the most advanced AI research and expertise, which in turn strengthens its AI offerings and competitive position. For Anthropic, the partnership provides the necessary resources and infrastructure to scale their innovations, bringing their pioneering AI models to a broader market and enabling more impactful applications.

In essence, the collaboration between Amazon and Anthropic exemplifies the power of strategic partnerships in driving AI innovation. By leveraging each other's strengths and fostering a collaborative environment, both companies have achieved remarkable advancements that enhance their AI capabilities and extend their influence in the industry. This partnership not only accelerates the development of sophisticated AI technologies but also ensures that these advancements are aligned with ethical standards and practical applications, ultimately benefiting businesses and consumers alike.

As Amazon continues to deepen its ties with Anthropic and explore new collaborative opportunities, the potential for further breakthroughs remains immense. These joint endeavors are poised to shape the future of artificial intelligence, setting new benchmarks for what is possible and reinforcing Amazon's position as a leading force in the AI arena. Through such collaborative innovations, Amazon is not just keeping pace with the rapidly evolving AI landscape; it is actively shaping its trajectory, driving forward a vision of a smarter, more efficient, and ethically sound technological future.

Chapter 4: Integrating AI Across Amazon's Operations

Amazon's approach to customer service has undergone a remarkable transformation, evolving from the rigid, rule-based chatbots of the past to the dynamic, conversational generative AI systems of today. Initially, Amazon deployed chatbots that operated on static decision trees, requiring customers to input numerous commands before receiving any meaningful assistance. These early systems were functional but often frustrating, as they lacked the ability to understand nuanced queries or anticipate customer needs effectively.

Recognizing the limitations of these early chatbots, Amazon embarked on a journey to revolutionize its customer service experience. The introduction of generative AI marked a pivotal shift, enabling more natural and intuitive interactions between customers and the support system. This new generation of AI-powered chatbots could comprehend context, interpret intent, and generate responses that felt genuinely conversational. For instance, when a customer reached out with a simple return request, the advanced chatbot could not only process the return swiftly but also predict potential issues based on recent purchases and offer proactive solutions.

The implementation of generative AI in customer service had a profound impact on customer satisfaction. With the enhanced ability to understand and respond to inquiries accurately, customers experienced quicker resolutions and a more personalized service. The AI-driven chatbots could handle a broader range of queries without escalating them to human agents, reducing wait times and increasing overall efficiency. This seamless interaction fostered a sense of reliability and trust among customers, knowing that their issues could be resolved promptly and effectively without the frustrations of navigating through cumbersome menus or repetitive information requests.

Operational efficiency also saw significant improvements as a result of this technological advancement. The generative AI systems could manage a higher volume of interactions simultaneously, ensuring that customer service operations remained smooth even during peak times. By automating routine tasks and inquiries, Amazon was able to allocate human resources to more complex and specialized issues, optimizing the workforce and reducing operational costs. Additionally, the AI's ability to analyze patterns in customer interactions provided valuable insights into common pain points and emerging trends, allowing Amazon to proactively address potential challenges and continuously enhance the customer experience.

Moreover, the integration of generative AI into customer service operations facilitated a more data-driven approach to decision-making. The AI systems could gather and process vast amounts of data from customer interactions, providing actionable intelligence that informed service strategies and business decisions. This data-centric methodology enabled Amazon to refine its customer service processes, ensuring that they remained aligned with evolving customer expectations and market demands.

The success of this transformation is evident in the substantial increase in customer satisfaction scores and the overall efficiency of Amazon's customer service operations. Customers benefited from faster, more accurate responses and a more engaging interaction, while Amazon enjoyed streamlined operations and reduced costs. This synergy between customer satisfaction and operational efficiency underscores the transformative power of generative AI in redefining the landscape of customer service.

In essence, Amazon's evolution from static chatbots to sophisticated generative AI systems exemplifies the company's commitment to leveraging cutting-edge technology to enhance every aspect of its business. By prioritizing both customer satisfaction and operational efficiency, Amazon has set a new standard for customer service in the digital age, demonstrating how intelligent systems can drive meaningful improvements and foster long-term loyalty among customers.

Amazon's dedication to fostering a thriving marketplace extends beyond enhancing customer experiences—it deeply invests in empowering its vast network of sellers. With over two million vendors contributing to more than sixty percent of the products sold on its platform worldwide, Amazon recognizes that the ease and efficiency with which sellers can list their products are paramount to maintaining its competitive edge.

Traditionally, the process for sellers to list a product on Amazon was intricate and time-consuming. They were required to navigate through lengthy forms filled with numerous fields, each designed to ensure that customers could easily find and understand the products they were interested in. While this meticulous approach aimed to enhance the shopping experience, it posed a significant challenge for sellers who had to dedicate considerable time and effort to complete these listings accurately.

Acknowledging the need for a more streamlined solution, Amazon introduced advanced AI tools specifically designed to simplify the product listing process. By leveraging generative AI, Amazon revolutionized how sellers input their product information. Instead of manually filling out extensive forms, sellers now have the option to provide just a few descriptive words, upload a picture, or share a URL related to their product. The AI-driven tool intelligently fills in the necessary attributes, such as product details, specifications, and categorization, with remarkable accuracy and speed.

This innovation has transformed the seller experience in profound ways. The reduced complexity and time required to list products have made it significantly easier for sellers to bring their offerings to market. As a result, Amazon has seen a substantial increase in the number of vendors willing to join and expand their presence on the platform. Over half a million sellers have already adopted these generative AI tools, benefiting from the enhanced efficiency and reduced administrative burden.

Moreover, by automating the product listing process, Amazon ensures that the information presented to customers is consistent, accurate, and optimized for searchability. This not only improves the overall quality of the marketplace but also boosts customer satisfaction by making it easier to find and purchase products that meet their needs. Sellers, on the other hand, can focus more on their core business activities—such as sourcing products, managing inventory, and engaging with customers—rather than getting bogged down by tedious data entry tasks.

The integration of AI tools into the seller ecosystem exemplifies Amazon's commitment to innovation and support for its partners. By making the listing process more intuitive and less labor-intensive, Amazon not only enhances the operational efficiency of its sellers but also attracts a broader range of vendors to its platform. This continuous improvement fosters a more dynamic and diverse marketplace, ensuring that Amazon remains a preferred destination for both sellers and shoppers alike.

In essence, Amazon's implementation of AI-driven tools for automating product listings is a strategic move that strengthens its marketplace by making it more accessible and attractive to sellers. This initiative underscores the company's broader vision of leveraging technology to create a seamless and efficient ecosystem where businesses of all sizes can thrive, ultimately driving sustained growth and innovation within the Amazon community.

Within these intricate supply chains, predicting what customers will want, when they will want it, and how best to deliver it has always been a complex challenge. The introduction of advanced Transformer models brought a profound shift in how Amazon approached demand forecasting. Instead of relying on older methods that struggled to account for changing trends, these new models uncovered patterns that were previously hidden, leading to far more reliable projections. Even subtle factors like regional buying habits or sudden shifts in seasonal demand could now be anticipated with striking precision. There was a marked improvement in long-term forecasting accuracy, a notable increase in the reliability of regional predictions, and a more efficient distribution of goods across fulfillment centers. By positioning items closer to customers who were more likely to order them, the entire operation became leaner and more responsive, ultimately lowering costs and reducing delivery times. The same spirit of innovation extended to the physical aspects of order fulfillment as well. Within the buzzing landscape of fulfillment centers, a new generation of AI-driven robotics emerged, most famously represented by a system called Sparrow. Rather than relying solely on human workers for the intricate task of sorting and rearranging inventory, Sparrow brought an unprecedented level of speed and consistency to the process. Guided by AI, it understood what needed to be moved, knew precisely how to handle each item, and deftly placed products into their proper locations. This increased velocity and precision in handling inventory freed human workers from routine tasks, allowing them to focus on more challenging responsibilities while simultaneously cutting down on operational expenses. The end result was a more nimble operation, one where shelves remained stocked with the right products at the right times, logistics ran more smoothly, and the workforce operated more efficiently. Such advances created a direct impact not only on cost savings and customer satisfaction but also on the broader ecosystem of vendors and sellers who depended on these platforms to reach their customers with speed and reliability.

Chapter 5: Innovative Shopping Experiences

Imagine browsing through an extensive online store, faced with countless choices and endless details about each product. For many, this can be overwhelming, making it difficult to find exactly what they need or to make informed decisions quickly. Recognizing this challenge, Amazon introduced Rufus, an AI-powered shopping agent designed to transform the way customers interact with products and make purchasing decisions.

Rufus acts as a personal assistant within the Amazon app, seamlessly integrating into product detail pages to provide real-time, personalized support. Instead of sifting through pages of specifications, customer reviews, and comparison charts, shoppers can simply ask Rufus any question they have about a product. Whether it's comparing different models, understanding specific features, or checking the status of an order, Rufus delivers clear and concise answers instantly. This eliminates the frustration of navigating complex menus or repeating information, streamlining the shopping experience significantly.

One of Rufus's standout features is its ability to make intelligent comparisons across products and categories. If a customer is torn between two similar items, Rufus can highlight the key differences, helping them understand which product better suits their needs. For example, if someone is deciding between two types of golf gloves, Rufus can pull up past purchase history and preferences to recommend the one that aligns best with their previous choices. This level of personalization ensures that each recommendation is tailored to the individual, enhancing the overall shopping experience.

Furthermore, Rufus is designed to anticipate customer needs by asking clarifying questions. If a shopper mentions they are looking for a specific feature or have particular preferences, Rufus can narrow down the options by asking targeted questions, much like a knowledgeable salesperson in a physical store. This interactive approach not only saves time but also builds a more engaging and satisfying shopping journey. For instance, if a customer is interested in purchasing a new laptop but is unsure about the specifications they need, Rufus can guide them through the necessary details, ensuring they make an informed decision without feeling overwhelmed.

Rufus also excels in providing real-time updates and support. Customers can inquire about the status of their orders, track shipments, or get assistance with returns directly through Rufus. This level of integration ensures that all aspects of the shopping process are handled efficiently within a single interface, reducing the need for customers to switch between different support channels.

By incorporating Rufus into the shopping experience, Amazon not only enhances customer satisfaction but also drives operational efficiency. Rufus reduces the load on human customer service agents by handling routine inquiries and tasks, allowing human representatives to focus on more complex issues. This balance ensures that customers receive timely and accurate support, while Amazon maintains high standards of service without escalating operational costs.

The introduction of Rufus signifies Amazon's commitment to leveraging artificial intelligence to create more intuitive and user-friendly shopping environments. By providing personalized assistance, intelligent recommendations, and seamless support, Rufus transforms the traditional online shopping model into a more interactive and engaging experience. Customers benefit from a smoother, more efficient journey, while Amazon strengthens its position as a leader in innovative retail solutions. Rufus exemplifies how AI can be harnessed to enhance everyday interactions, making online shopping not only easier but also more enjoyable for millions of users worldwide.

Amazon has always been at the forefront of innovation, constantly seeking ways to enhance the shopping experience for its vast customer base. One of the most remarkable advancements in this pursuit is Amazon Lens, a cutting-edge visual search technology that is revolutionizing how customers discover and interact with products. By harnessing the power of computer vision, Amazon Lens transforms the traditional online shopping paradigm, making product discovery more intuitive, engaging, and efficient.

Imagine strolling through a friend's home and spotting a stylish planter that catches your eye. In the past, identifying and purchasing such an item would require a series of manual searches and endless browsing through online catalogs. With Amazon Lens, this process becomes seamless and almost magical. By simply taking a picture of the planter using the Amazon app, Lens employs sophisticated computer vision algorithms to analyze the image, recognize the product, and instantly provide relevant search results. This capability bridges the gap between the physical and digital shopping experiences, allowing customers to effortlessly find and purchase items that match their tastes and needs without the tedious process of manual searching.

The transformative impact of computer vision extends beyond mere product identification. Amazon Lens enhances product discovery by understanding the context and nuances of what customers are looking for. For instance, if a customer is searching for a specific type of furniture or a unique gadget, Lens can interpret the visual cues from the uploaded image and suggest similar or complementary products. This not only saves time but also introduces customers to items they might not have discovered otherwise, enriching their shopping journey with personalized and relevant recommendations.

Real-world applications of Amazon Lens demonstrate its versatility and effectiveness across various scenarios. In the fashion industry, customers can use Lens to find clothing items that match a particular style or pattern seen in a photograph, ensuring they find the perfect fit and design without guesswork. In the realm of home decor, Lens allows users to replicate the aesthetic of a favorite piece seen in a magazine or a friend's house, providing exact matches or comparable alternatives available on Amazon's platform. Additionally, for tech enthusiasts, Lens can identify and suggest the latest gadgets and accessories based on images of products they admire, keeping them updated with the latest trends and innovations.

User experiences with Amazon Lens have been overwhelmingly positive, with many praising its accuracy and ease of use. Customers appreciate the ability to quickly locate products without the hassle of navigating through extensive search filters or reading lengthy descriptions. The instant visual recognition fosters a more engaging and satisfying shopping experience, as users feel more connected to the products they choose. Moreover, the integration of Lens into the Amazon app ensures that this powerful tool is readily accessible, encouraging more interactive and dynamic interactions between customers and the platform.

Another significant advancement in Amazon's AI-driven initiatives is the introduction of AI-Powered Size Recommendations. One of the persistent challenges in online retail, particularly in the apparel industry, is ensuring that customers select the correct size, thereby reducing the rate of returns and enhancing overall satisfaction. Amazon addresses this issue by leveraging extensive customer data and advanced AI algorithms to provide personalized sizing recommendations that are both accurate and reliable.

Reducing return rates through precise sizing is a win-win situation for both customers and sellers. For customers, accurate size recommendations mean fewer mismatches between their expectations and the actual product, leading to a more satisfying purchase experience. For sellers, lower return rates translate to reduced operational costs and improved inventory management. Amazon's AI-Powered Size Recommendations analyze a multitude of factors, including past purchase history, customer feedback, and specific product measurements, to offer tailored size suggestions that align perfectly with each individual's unique body measurements and preferences.

By meticulously analyzing customer data, Amazon's AI can discern patterns and preferences that might not be immediately apparent. For example, if a customer consistently orders a particular size in one brand but prefers a slightly different fit in another, the AI can adjust its recommendations accordingly. This level of personalization ensures that each recommendation is not only based on general sizing standards but also finely tuned to the customer's specific needs and past behaviors. The result is a more accurate and trustworthy sizing guide that enhances the overall shopping experience and fosters greater customer loyalty.

Leveraging customer data for personalized recommendations goes beyond just sizing. Amazon's AI systems delve deep into individual preferences, shopping habits, and even style choices to offer a comprehensive and personalized shopping experience. This data-driven approach allows Amazon to anticipate customer needs and present them with products that are not only relevant but also aligned with their personal tastes and requirements. Whether it's suggesting a size that fits better, recommending a color that complements a customer's wardrobe, or highlighting products that match their lifestyle, Amazon's AI ensures that each interaction is meaningful and valuable.

The integration of AI-Powered Size Recommendations exemplifies Amazon's commitment to using technology to solve real-world problems and enhance customer satisfaction. By addressing the common pain points associated with online shopping, Amazon not only improves the user experience but also strengthens its position as a leader in innovative retail solutions. This initiative highlights how AI can be harnessed to create smarter, more efficient, and more customer-centric shopping environments, ultimately driving sustained growth and loyalty in an increasingly competitive market.

In essence, Amazon Lens and AI-Powered Size Recommendations are prime examples of how Amazon leverages artificial intelligence to transform the shopping journey. These technologies not only simplify product discovery and sizing but also create a more personalized and satisfying experience for customers. By continuously innovating and integrating advanced AI capabilities into its platform, Amazon ensures that it remains at the cutting edge of retail technology, setting new standards for what customers can expect from their online shopping experiences. These initiatives underscore Amazon's unwavering dedication to using AI to enhance every aspect of its business, driving both customer satisfaction and operational excellence in a harmonious and forward-thinking manner.

Chapter 6: Amazon's Foray into AI Hardware

Amazon's relentless pursuit of technological supremacy led to the ambitious development of the Ultra Cluster Supercomputer, a monumental step in redefining the boundaries of artificial intelligence. This state-of-the-art supercomputer is not merely a collection of high-performance machines; it represents Amazon's strategic vision to build an AI infrastructure that rivals, and potentially surpasses, existing industry standards. The Ultra Cluster is designed to handle the immense computational demands of modern AI applications, providing the backbone for training and deploying sophisticated AI models that drive Amazon's diverse range of services.

At the heart of the Ultra Cluster lies the Tranium chip, Amazon's proprietary AI processor. These chips are meticulously engineered to optimize performance, efficiency, and scalability, addressing the specific needs of large-scale AI operations.

Unlike off-the-shelf GPUs, the Tranium chips are tailored to seamlessly integrate with Amazon's unique infrastructure, ensuring that the Ultra Cluster operates at peak efficiency. This custom hardware allows Amazon to fine-tune its AI capabilities, reducing latency and increasing processing speeds, which are critical factors in delivering real-time, responsive AI services to millions of users worldwide.

The significance of the Tranium chips extends beyond their technical specifications. By developing their own AI processors, Amazon gains unprecedented control over its hardware ecosystem, mitigating dependencies on external suppliers like Nvidia. This vertical integration not only enhances Amazon's ability to innovate rapidly but also provides a strategic advantage in negotiating costs and ensuring a steady supply of essential components. The Ultra Cluster, powered by Tranium chips, exemplifies Amazon's commitment to building a resilient and scalable AI infrastructure that can adapt to the evolving demands of the technology landscape.

Moreover, the Ultra Cluster's capabilities are a testament to Amazon's foresight in anticipating the future of AI. With hundreds of thousands of Tranium-powered servers, the Ultra Cluster stands as one of the largest AI supercomputers in the world, designed to train expansive AI models that require vast amounts of data and computational power. This immense scale allows Amazon to push the envelope in AI research and development, fostering innovations that can drive advancements across various sectors, from e-commerce and logistics to entertainment and cloud computing.

The Ultra Cluster also plays a crucial role in Amazon's broader AI strategy by enabling the company to offer competitive AI services through Amazon Web Services (AWS). By providing customers with access to this powerful infrastructure, Amazon empowers businesses of all sizes to develop and deploy their own AI solutions with greater ease and efficiency. This democratization of AI technology not only broadens AWS's appeal but also solidifies Amazon's position as a leader in the cloud-based AI services market.

In essence, the creation of the Ultra Cluster Supercomputer and the development of Tranium chips signify a pivotal moment in Amazon's journey towards AI dominance. These innovations reflect the company's dedication to building a robust and versatile AI infrastructure that can support its extensive range of services and meet the growing demands of the digital age. By investing in proprietary hardware and scalable supercomputing capabilities, Amazon is not only enhancing its own operational efficiency but also paving the way for future advancements that will shape the landscape of artificial intelligence for years to come.

Amazon's strategic ambition to reshape the artificial intelligence landscape extends beyond software and services; it boldly ventures into the hardware domain, directly challenging the longstanding dominance of Nvidia in the GPU market. Nvidia has long been synonymous with high-performance graphics processing units, which are integral to AI computations, gaming, and professional visualization. However, Amazon's innovative approach seeks to diversify the hardware options available to AI developers and enterprises, thereby fostering a more competitive and dynamic market.

At the core of Amazon's strategy to offer alternatives to Nvidia's GPUs lies the development of its proprietary AI chips, the Tranium series. These chips are meticulously designed to cater specifically to the demands of large-scale AI operations, optimizing performance, energy efficiency, and scalability. By creating their own hardware, Amazon gains the flexibility to tailor the chips precisely to their AI workloads, reducing latency and increasing computational throughput in ways that off-the-shelf GPUs may not achieve. This customization allows Amazon to fine-tune their AI infrastructure, ensuring that it aligns perfectly with their operational needs and performance benchmarks.

In addition to developing custom chips, Amazon is investing heavily in the construction of supercomputing infrastructure like the Ultra Cluster. This massive AI supercomputer, powered by Tranium chips, not only serves Amazon's internal needs but also forms the backbone of their AI services offered through Amazon Web Services (AWS). By providing these advanced hardware solutions to their extensive customer base, Amazon positions itself as a formidable alternative to Nvidia, offering scalable and cost-effective options for businesses looking to deploy AI at scale. This move not only diversifies the hardware ecosystem but also empowers more companies to innovate without being tethered to a single GPU provider.

The implications of Amazon's challenge to Nvidia's dominance are profound for the AI hardware market. A more competitive environment spurs innovation, driving the development of more efficient, powerful, and affordable hardware solutions. This competition can lead to faster advancements in AI technology, as companies strive to outdo each other in terms of performance and capabilities. For consumers and businesses alike, this means access to a broader range of options, potentially lower costs, and enhanced performance from the hardware that powers their AI applications.

Moreover, Amazon's entry into the GPU market disrupts the existing power dynamics, providing customers with alternatives that may better suit their specific needs. For instance, enterprises that require highly specialized AI computations might find Amazon's custom hardware more aligned with their operational requirements than traditional Nvidia GPUs. This shift not only reduces the monopoly that Nvidia enjoys but also encourages other tech giants to innovate and diversify their hardware offerings, fostering a healthier and more resilient AI ecosystem.

Looking ahead, the future prospects of Amazon's AI infrastructure are both expansive and promising. The scalability of their AI solutions, underpinned by proprietary hardware and robust cloud services, positions Amazon to capture a significant share of the growing AI market. As AI applications continue to proliferate across various industries—from healthcare and finance to entertainment and logistics—Amazon's infrastructure is poised to support these diverse and demanding use cases with unparalleled efficiency and reliability.

The potential market impact of Amazon's AI infrastructure is substantial. By offering a comprehensive suite of AI tools and hardware, Amazon can attract a wide array of customers, from startups to multinational corporations, each seeking to harness the power of AI to drive innovation and competitive advantage. This broad appeal ensures that Amazon remains at the forefront of the AI revolution, continuously expanding its influence and market presence. Additionally, the integration of AI hardware with their existing services creates a seamless ecosystem that enhances user experience and operational synergy, making it easier for businesses to adopt and scale AI solutions without the complexities of managing disparate systems.

In the long term, the benefits of Amazon's AI infrastructure for both the company and its customers are multifaceted. For Amazon, the development of proprietary AI hardware and scalable infrastructure solidifies its position as a leader in the AI domain, driving sustained growth and technological leadership. It also opens new revenue streams through the sale and licensing of their hardware and AI services, further diversifying their business model and enhancing financial stability.

For customers, Amazon's AI infrastructure offers enhanced performance, greater flexibility, and cost-effective solutions tailored to their specific needs. Businesses can leverage Amazon's advanced hardware and AI models to optimize their operations, innovate new products and services, and gain deeper insights from their data. This empowerment fosters a more dynamic and competitive business environment, where companies can thrive by effectively utilizing cutting-edge AI technologies.

Ultimately, Amazon's bold move to challenge Nvidia's dominance in the AI hardware market exemplifies their commitment to driving innovation and shaping the future of artificial intelligence. By offering alternatives to traditional GPU providers, Amazon not only enhances its own AI capabilities but also contributes to a more diverse and competitive hardware ecosystem. This strategic initiative ensures that Amazon remains a pivotal force in the AI landscape, continuously pushing the boundaries of what is possible and delivering transformative value to businesses and consumers worldwide.

Chapter 7: Market Perception and Stock Performance

Amazon's strategic advancements in artificial intelligence have significantly bolstered investor confidence, reflecting the company's unwavering commitment to innovation and market leadership. Following the series of high-profile AI announcements, including the launch of Amazon Nova and the development of the Ultra Cluster Supercomputer, Amazon's stock performance has shown a marked uptick. Investors have responded positively to these initiatives, recognizing the potential for sustained growth and enhanced profitability driven by cutting-edge AI technologies. The stock's rise is a testament to the market's acknowledgment of Amazon's ability to leverage its extensive infrastructure and technological prowess to stay ahead in the competitive AI landscape.

Several factors contribute to this surge in investor optimism. Firstly, Amazon's comprehensive approach to integrating AI across its diverse range of services—from e-commerce and logistics to cloud computing and entertainment—demonstrates a robust and scalable business model. This integration not only enhances operational efficiency but also creates new revenue streams, positioning Amazon to capitalize on the growing demand for AI-driven solutions. Investors are particularly impressed by Amazon's ability to innovate continuously, as seen in the deployment of specialized AI models within the Nova suite and the strategic partnerships with leading AI research firms like Anthropic. These collaborations ensure that Amazon remains at the forefront of AI advancements, fostering a culture of innovation that drives long-term value.

Additionally, Amazon's investment in proprietary AI hardware, such as the Tranium chips and the Ultra Cluster Supercomputer, signals a strategic move to reduce dependency on external suppliers and control the entire AI development pipeline. This vertical integration not only enhances performance and cost-efficiency but also provides Amazon with a competitive edge in the AI hardware market. By challenging established players like Nvidia, Amazon is not only diversifying its technological assets but also positioning itself as a formidable contender capable of shaping the future of AI infrastructure. This proactive stance reassures investors of Amazon's resilience and adaptability in an ever-evolving technological landscape.

Moreover, the tangible improvements in customer service and operational efficiency, driven by AI innovations like generative chatbots and AI-powered logistics, translate directly into enhanced profitability and customer satisfaction. These advancements reduce operational costs, streamline processes, and create a more seamless and engaging customer experience, all of which contribute to stronger financial performance. The ability to anticipate and meet customer needs more effectively through AI-driven insights further solidifies Amazon's market position, making it an attractive investment prospect.

The positive stock performance is also fueled by Amazon's strategic vision for the future, where AI plays a central role in driving growth and maintaining competitive dominance. Investors are keenly aware of the transformative potential of AI and recognize Amazon's efforts to harness this technology as a catalyst for sustained expansion. The company's ability to anticipate market trends, invest in future-proof technologies, and execute its AI strategy with precision instills a sense of confidence among investors, who see Amazon as a forward-thinking leader capable of navigating and shaping the future of multiple industries.

In summary, Amazon's ambitious AI initiatives have not only advanced its technological capabilities but also significantly enhanced investor confidence. The combination of robust AI integration, strategic hardware investments, innovative partnerships, and tangible operational improvements creates a compelling narrative of growth and resilience. As Amazon continues to push the boundaries of artificial intelligence, its stock performance remains a reflection of the market's belief in the company's ability to deliver long-term value and maintain its leadership position in the global technology landscape.

As the landscape of technology continues to evolve at an unprecedented pace, so too do the narratives that define the identities of leading corporations. Amazon, long celebrated as an e-commerce titan and a powerhouse in cloud computing, has undergone a remarkable transformation in the eyes of the investment community. This shift from being perceived solely as an online retail giant to emerging as a formidable leader in artificial intelligence underscores the company's strategic agility and forward-thinking vision.

Historically, Amazon's reputation was firmly rooted in its ability to revolutionize online shopping and dominate the cloud services market through

Amazon Web Services (AWS). Investors admired the company's relentless expansion, efficient logistics, and customer-centric approach, which consistently translated into robust financial performance and steady stock growth. However, as the global economy increasingly embraces digital transformation and automation, the focus has begun to pivot towards the underlying technologies that drive these changes. In this context, Amazon's foray into artificial intelligence has redefined its standing, prompting a reevaluation of its potential and value within the investment community.

The infusion of AI into Amazon's core operations has been a game-changer, altering perceptions and enhancing investor confidence. With the launch of Amazon Nova and the development of proprietary AI hardware like the Tranium chips and the Ultra Cluster Supercomputer, Amazon has positioned itself at the forefront of AI innovation. These initiatives signal a deliberate move to harness AI not just as a tool for optimization but as a cornerstone of its future growth strategy. Investors, keenly attuned to the transformative power of AI, have responded positively to these advancements, recognizing the potential for Amazon to lead in a technology that is set to redefine multiple industries.

This strategic pivot has had a tangible impact on Amazon's market valuation. The company's stock performance has seen a notable uptick following key AI announcements and milestones. Analysts attribute this rise to the enhanced growth prospects that AI integration brings, envisioning Amazon not just as a steady performer in e-commerce and cloud computing but as a dynamic innovator in the AI sector. The anticipation of sustained revenue growth from AI-driven services, coupled with the potential for new business models and revenue streams, has fueled investor optimism. This positive sentiment is reflected in the increasing market capitalization and the elevated stock prices, underscoring the market's confidence in Amazon's ability to leverage AI for long-term success.

Moreover, Amazon's comprehensive approach to AI—from developing versatile generative models and advanced robotics to creating specialized AI hardware—demonstrates a holistic vision that resonates with investors looking for diversified and resilient growth. The company's ability to integrate AI seamlessly into its vast ecosystem enhances operational efficiencies, reduces costs, and improves customer experiences, all of which are critical factors that contribute to its robust financial health. Investors are particularly impressed by Amazon's proactive stance in building an AI infrastructure that not only supports its existing services but also paves the way for future innovations and market expansions.

The changing narrative around Amazon is also influenced by its strategic partnerships and collaborations in the AI domain. By deepening ties with leading AI research firms like Anthropic,

Amazon ensures access to cutting-edge technologies and expertise, further solidifying its leadership position. These alliances not only enhance Amazon's AI capabilities but also demonstrate the company's commitment to fostering innovation through collaboration. Such strategic moves are viewed favorably by investors, who see them as indicators of Amazon's ability to stay ahead of technological trends and maintain its competitive edge.

In essence, the investment community's evolving perception of Amazon from an e-commerce behemoth to an AI leader is a reflection of the company's strategic initiatives and technological advancements. The integration of AI into Amazon's business model has unlocked new avenues for growth, efficiency, and innovation, making the company an increasingly attractive proposition for investors. As Amazon continues to push the boundaries of what artificial intelligence can achieve, its market valuation is poised to benefit from the enhanced growth prospects and the promise of sustained leadership in a technology that is reshaping the global economy.

This transformation is not merely about adding another facet to Amazon's already impressive portfolio; it signifies a fundamental reimagining of the company's role in the future of technology. By embracing AI as a central pillar of its strategy, Amazon is not only ensuring its relevance in an increasingly automated world but also setting new standards for what it means to be a technology leader. For investors, this shift represents a compelling narrative of innovation, resilience, and strategic foresight, solidifying Amazon's position as a powerhouse poised to thrive in the age of artificial intelligence.

Chapter 8: Comparative Analysis with Other AI Leaders

Salesforce has long been a cornerstone in the realm of customer relationship management, providing businesses with the tools they need to manage interactions, analyze data, and drive sales. However, as the technological landscape rapidly evolves, Salesforce has adeptly positioned itself at the forefront of artificial intelligence innovation, introducing groundbreaking solutions that extend far beyond traditional CRM functionalities. One of the most notable advancements in Salesforce's AI portfolio is the introduction of Agent Force, a sophisticated AI-driven agent designed to revolutionize the way businesses operate and interact with their customers.

Agent Force represents a significant leap forward in Salesforce's AI strategy, embodying the company's commitment to enhancing operational efficiency and delivering unparalleled value to its clients. Unlike conventional chatbots that handle basic queries and repetitive tasks, Agent Force is engineered to undertake complex, multifaceted responsibilities that typically require human intelligence and decision-making. This AI agent is capable of performing entire human tasks, from managing intricate workflows to executing strategic initiatives, thereby reducing the burden on human employees and allowing them to focus on more creative and high-level endeavors.

The introduction of Agent Force has been met with remarkable enthusiasm from Salesforce's extensive customer base. Within its first week of deployment, over 200 customers signed up for the service, a testament to the high demand for advanced AI solutions that can drive significant efficiency gains. These early adopters have reported substantial improvements in their operational workflows, as Agent Force seamlessly integrates into existing systems to automate processes, analyze data, and provide actionable insights. By doing so, Agent Force not only streamlines daily operations but also enhances the overall productivity and effectiveness of businesses across various industries.

A key feature of Agent Force is its ability to lower the intensity of work required for companies' employees. By automating monotonous and time-consuming tasks, Agent Force alleviates the strain on human workers, enabling them to concentrate on more strategic and impactful activities. This shift not only boosts employee morale and job satisfaction but also leads to higher retention rates and a more motivated workforce. Furthermore, Agent Force promises remarkable efficiency gains, as businesses can accomplish more with fewer resources, ultimately driving down operational costs and increasing profitability.

Salesforce's approach to AI with Agent Force highlights a strategic vision that prioritizes both innovation and practicality. The AI agent is designed to be highly adaptable, capable of handling a wide range of tasks across different departments and functions. Whether it's automating customer service inquiries, managing sales pipelines, or optimizing marketing campaigns, Agent Force provides a versatile solution that can be tailored to meet the unique needs of each business. This flexibility ensures that Salesforce's AI innovations are not only cutting-edge but also highly relevant and applicable to real-world business challenges.

When comparing Salesforce's AI strategies to those of Amazon, several key differences and similarities emerge. Both companies recognize the transformative potential of artificial intelligence and have invested heavily in developing AI-driven solutions that enhance their core offerings. However, their approaches reflect their distinct business models and strategic priorities.

Amazon's AI strategy is deeply integrated into its expansive ecosystem, spanning e-commerce, cloud computing, logistics, and entertainment. The launch of Amazon Nova and the development of proprietary AI hardware like the Tranium chips underscore Amazon's commitment to building a comprehensive AI infrastructure that supports a wide range of applications. Amazon leverages its vast data resources and cloud infrastructure to deliver scalable and versatile AI solutions, aiming to dominate multiple facets of the technology landscape.

In contrast, Salesforce's AI initiatives are more focused on enhancing its CRM platform and providing specialized tools that directly benefit its customer base. Agent Force exemplifies this approach by targeting specific business functions and offering tailored solutions that drive efficiency and productivity. While Amazon emphasizes broad integration and infrastructure development, Salesforce concentrates on creating highly specialized AI tools that deliver immediate and measurable value to its users.

Despite these differences, both companies share a common goal of using AI to drive innovation and improve business outcomes. They both understand that the key to successful AI adoption lies in creating solutions that are not only technologically advanced but also user-friendly and directly aligned with the needs of their customers. By focusing on different aspects of AI, Amazon and Salesforce complement each other in the broader AI ecosystem, each contributing to the advancement of artificial intelligence in unique and meaningful ways.

Moreover, both Amazon and Salesforce recognize the importance of strategic partnerships in enhancing their AI capabilities. Amazon's collaboration with Anthropic and Salesforce's partnerships within the tech industry illustrate their commitment to leveraging external expertise and fostering a culture of continuous innovation. These alliances enable both companies to stay ahead of technological trends, ensuring that their AI solutions remain cutting-edge and highly competitive in a rapidly evolving market.

In summary, Salesforce's introduction of Agent Force marks a significant milestone in the company's AI journey, showcasing its ability to innovate and deliver impactful solutions that enhance business operations. When compared to Amazon's broader AI strategies, Salesforce's focused approach highlights the diverse ways in which leading tech companies are harnessing the power of artificial intelligence. Both companies, through their unique strategies and innovations, are shaping the future of AI, driving efficiency, and creating value for businesses worldwide. As AI continues to evolve, the synergy between specialized tools like Agent Force and comprehensive AI infrastructures like Amazon Nova will play a crucial role in defining the next era of technological advancement and business excellence.

The competition between Nvidia and Amazon in the GPU market has become one of the most intriguing battles in the technology sector. Nvidia has long been synonymous with high-performance graphics processing units, which are not only essential for gaming and professional visualization but have also become the backbone of many artificial intelligence applications. Their GPUs are renowned for their unparalleled processing power and efficiency, making them the preferred choice for researchers, developers, and enterprises worldwide. Nvidia's dominance in the GPU market is underpinned by its continuous innovation, robust ecosystem, and strategic partnerships that have solidified its position as the industry leader.

Amazon, traditionally known for its prowess in e-commerce and cloud computing through Amazon Web Services (AWS), has been making significant strides to challenge Nvidia's supremacy in the GPU arena. Recognizing the critical role that specialized hardware plays in the advancement of AI, Amazon has embarked on a mission to develop its own AI chips, the Tranium series, and build comprehensive AI infrastructure like the Ultra Cluster

Supercomputer. This strategic move is aimed at reducing Amazon's reliance on external GPU suppliers and creating a more integrated and cost-effective solution tailored to its specific needs.

Nvidia's approach has always been centered around pushing the boundaries of GPU technology. Their commitment to research and development has led to the creation of GPUs that offer exceptional performance, power efficiency, and scalability. Nvidia's CUDA platform, which enables parallel computing, has become a standard in the industry, providing developers with the tools they need to harness the full potential of their hardware. Additionally, Nvidia has cultivated a vast ecosystem of software, libraries, and partnerships that enhance the functionality and applicability of their GPUs across various domains, from deep learning and data analytics to autonomous vehicles and virtual reality.

In contrast, Amazon's strategy is characterized by vertical integration and customization. By designing its own AI chips, Amazon gains complete control over the hardware lifecycle, from development to deployment. This allows Amazon to tailor its hardware specifically to the requirements of its AI models and services, optimizing performance and cost in ways that off-the-shelf GPUs might not achieve. The Ultra Cluster Supercomputer, powered by Tranium chips, exemplifies this approach, offering a scalable and efficient infrastructure that supports Amazon's expansive AI initiatives. This bespoke hardware solution not only enhances Amazon's internal operations but also provides a competitive edge in the cloud services market, where efficiency and scalability are paramount.

The market implications of Amazon's AI hardware initiatives are profound. By developing proprietary chips and building state-of-the-art supercomputers, Amazon is positioning itself as a serious contender in the AI hardware space, traditionally dominated by Nvidia. This move introduces a significant alternative for businesses and researchers who rely heavily on GPU technology for their AI workloads. With Amazon offering its own line of AI chips through AWS, customers now have the option to choose between Nvidia's proven GPUs and Amazon's customized solutions, fostering a more competitive and diverse hardware ecosystem.

Furthermore, Amazon's entry into the GPU market has the potential to drive down costs and spur innovation. As Amazon scales its AI hardware offerings, the increased competition is likely to lead to more affordable pricing and improved performance across the board. This not only benefits Amazon's customers by providing them with more options and better value but also challenges Nvidia to continue innovating and maintaining its technological edge. The resulting dynamic can accelerate advancements in GPU technology, benefiting the entire AI industry by enabling more powerful and efficient computing solutions.

Additionally, Amazon's strategic investments in AI hardware underscore the growing importance of specialized hardware in the advancement of artificial intelligence. As AI applications become more sophisticated and data-intensive, the demand for high-performance computing solutions continues to rise. Amazon's proactive approach in developing tailored hardware ensures that it is well-equipped to meet the evolving needs of the market, positioning itself to capture a significant share of the AI hardware segment. This forward-thinking strategy not only enhances Amazon's competitiveness but also drives the broader AI ecosystem towards greater innovation and efficiency.

The rivalry between Nvidia and Amazon also highlights the broader trends shaping the AI hardware market. As companies recognize the critical role of customized and scalable hardware in AI development, the focus is shifting towards creating solutions that are not only powerful but also adaptable to specific use cases. This shift is driving a new wave of innovation, where hardware is increasingly being designed to meet the unique demands of different AI applications, from natural language processing and computer vision to autonomous systems and beyond.

In the long run, Amazon's challenge to Nvidia's dominance is likely to have lasting effects on the AI hardware landscape. By introducing a viable alternative to Nvidia's GPUs, Amazon is fostering a more competitive environment that encourages continuous improvement and diversification of hardware solutions. This competition is essential for the healthy growth of the AI industry, as it ensures that advancements are not hindered by monopolistic practices and that a variety of needs and preferences are catered to.

For investors and stakeholders, the implications are equally significant. Amazon's foray into AI hardware signals the company's intent to lead not just in software and services but also in the foundational technologies that drive AI advancements. This comprehensive approach enhances Amazon's resilience and adaptability, making it a more attractive investment prospect as it diversifies its revenue streams and strengthens its technological capabilities. Investors can view Amazon's AI hardware initiatives as a strategic move that complements its existing strengths in cloud computing and AI services, positioning the company for sustained growth and leadership in the tech industry.

In summary, the GPU battle between Nvidia and Amazon epitomizes the dynamic and rapidly evolving nature of the AI hardware market. While Nvidia continues to set high standards with its cutting-edge GPU technology and expansive ecosystem, Amazon is carving out its own niche through vertical integration and customized hardware solutions. The competition between these two tech giants is not only reshaping their individual trajectories but also driving the broader

AI industry towards greater innovation, efficiency, and accessibility. As Amazon and Nvidia continue to push the boundaries of what is possible with GPU technology, the market stands to benefit from enhanced performance, reduced costs, and a more diverse array of options for businesses and researchers alike.

Chapter 9: Real-World Impact and Future Implications

Amazon's relentless pursuit of technological innovation has profoundly reshaped the customer experience, setting new standards for what consumers can expect from their interactions with one of the world's largest online retailers. By seamlessly integrating artificial intelligence into every facet of its operations, Amazon has not only enhanced the efficiency of its services but also created a more personalized and engaging shopping journey for its customers. This strategic infusion of AI has yielded long-term benefits that extend far beyond immediate conveniences, fundamentally transforming the way consumers shop, interact, and perceive value.

One of the most significant long-term benefits of Amazon's AI integration lies in the unparalleled personalization it offers. By analyzing vast amounts of data from customer interactions, purchase histories, and browsing behaviors, Amazon's AI systems can predict individual preferences with remarkable accuracy. This enables the platform to recommend products that are highly relevant to each user, creating a tailored shopping experience that feels uniquely personal. Over time, this level of customization fosters a deeper connection between the consumer and the platform, increasing customer loyalty and satisfaction. As AI continues to evolve, these personalized experiences become even more refined, anticipating needs and desires that customers may not have explicitly expressed, thereby enhancing their overall shopping journey.

Moreover, AI-driven enhancements in customer service have had a profound impact on operational efficiency and customer satisfaction. The transition from static, rule-based chatbots to sophisticated generative AI systems has revolutionized how Amazon handles customer inquiries and support requests. These advanced AI agents can understand and respond to complex queries in real-time, providing accurate and helpful solutions without the delays associated with human intervention. This not only reduces wait times but also ensures that customers receive consistent and reliable assistance, regardless of the time of day or the volume of requests. As a result, customers experience a smoother, more efficient support process, which significantly boosts their trust and confidence in Amazon's ability to meet their needs promptly and effectively.

The integration of AI into logistics and inventory management has also delivered substantial benefits to consumers by ensuring that products are available when and where they are needed most. Advanced demand forecasting models, powered by AI, allow Amazon to predict purchasing trends with high precision, enabling the company to maintain optimal inventory levels across its vast network of fulfillment centers. This proactive approach minimizes the risk of stockouts and reduces delivery times, ensuring that customers receive their orders faster and more reliably. Additionally,

AI-driven logistics optimizations streamline the supply chain, lowering operational costs and enabling Amazon to offer competitive pricing, which directly benefits consumers through more affordable products and faster delivery options.

Real-world case studies vividly illustrate the tangible improvements that Amazon's AI initiatives have brought to the customer experience. For instance, the deployment of AI-powered chatbots in Amazon's customer service operations has led to a significant increase in customer satisfaction scores. By handling routine inquiries and providing instant responses, these chatbots free up human agents to focus on more complex and nuanced issues, enhancing the overall quality of support. Customers appreciate the efficiency and accuracy of these AI systems, which resolve their concerns swiftly and effectively, leading to a more positive perception of Amazon's customer service capabilities.

Another compelling example is the introduction of AI-driven size recommendation systems in

Amazon's apparel section. By analyzing customer data and understanding individual sizing preferences, Amazon's AI can accurately suggest the best size for each customer, significantly reducing the likelihood of returns due to sizing issues. This not only enhances the shopping experience by making it easier for customers to find the right fit but also reduces the environmental and financial costs associated with product returns. Customers benefit from a more reliable and hassle-free shopping process, while Amazon enjoys lower return rates and improved inventory management.

In the realm of entertainment, Amazon Prime Video leverages AI to offer personalized content recommendations that align with each user's viewing habits and preferences. By analyzing factors such as watch history, genre preferences, and even the time spent watching certain types of content, Prime Video's AI systems curate a tailored selection of movies and shows that are most likely to engage each viewer. This level of personalization ensures that users are continuously presented with content that resonates with their interests, enhancing their overall viewing experience and increasing their satisfaction with the service.

Furthermore, the implementation of AI-driven robotics in Amazon's fulfillment centers has revolutionized the efficiency and speed of order processing. Robots equipped with advanced AI capabilities can swiftly and accurately sort, pack, and ship products, reducing the time it takes for customers to receive their orders. This technological advancement not only improves the speed of delivery but also enhances the accuracy of order fulfillment, minimizing errors and ensuring that customers receive exactly what they ordered. The increased efficiency in fulfillment operations translates to faster delivery times and higher reliability, which are critical factors in maintaining customer satisfaction and loyalty.

The long-term benefits of these AI integrations are manifold, contributing to a more seamless and enjoyable shopping experience for consumers. As AI technologies continue to advance, Amazon is poised to further enhance its services, offering even more sophisticated and intuitive solutions that anticipate and meet the evolving needs of its customers. From personalized recommendations and efficient customer support to optimized logistics and innovative shopping tools, AI plays a pivotal role in driving Amazon's mission to deliver unparalleled value and convenience to its global customer base.

In conclusion, Amazon's strategic integration of artificial intelligence into its operations has fundamentally transformed the customer experience, delivering long-term benefits that enhance personalization, efficiency, and satisfaction. Through continuous innovation and the deployment of advanced AI technologies, Amazon not only meets the current needs of its customers but also anticipates and adapts to future demands, ensuring a consistently superior shopping experience. These AI-driven enhancements underscore Amazon's commitment to leveraging technology to create meaningful value for its customers, solidifying its position as a leader in the ever-evolving landscape of e-commerce and artificial intelligence.

Amazon's integration of artificial intelligence has not only revolutionized customer interactions but has also significantly enhanced the company's operational efficiency and driven substantial cost savings. By embedding AI into the very fabric of its operations, Amazon has transformed its business processes, enabling more precise decision-making, optimizing resource allocation, and streamlining workflows across its vast network.

One of the most tangible financial impacts of AI on Amazon's operations is the reduction in operational costs. Advanced AI algorithms analyze vast amounts of data in real-time, identifying inefficiencies and recommending actionable improvements. For instance, in inventory management, AI-driven demand forecasting models predict product demand with high accuracy, allowing Amazon to maintain optimal stock levels. This precision minimizes excess inventory, reduces storage costs, and decreases the likelihood of stockouts, ensuring that products are available to customers when needed without incurring unnecessary expenses.

Furthermore, AI has played a crucial role in optimizing Amazon's logistics and supply chain operations. By leveraging machine learning models, Amazon can determine the most efficient routes for its delivery fleet, reducing fuel consumption and transportation costs. These models take into account various factors such as traffic patterns, weather conditions, and delivery urgency, ensuring that packages reach their destinations in the shortest possible time while minimizing operational costs. The result is a more streamlined delivery process that enhances both speed and cost-effectiveness, contributing to Amazon's competitive edge in the e-commerce market.

Another area where AI has driven significant cost savings is in the automation of warehouse operations. AI-powered robotics, such as those seen in Amazon's fulfillment centers, automate repetitive and labor-intensive tasks like sorting, packing, and shipping products. These robots work alongside human employees, handling the bulk of the physical workload and allowing human workers to focus on more complex and value-added activities. This synergy between AI and human labor not only increases the overall efficiency of warehouse operations but also reduces labor costs and enhances productivity. The ability to process and fulfill orders more rapidly and accurately translates to lower operational costs and improved profit margins.

AI has also enhanced Amazon's ability to manage and analyze data, leading to more informed business decisions and strategic planning. By utilizing AI-driven analytics, Amazon can gain deeper insights into customer behavior, market trends, and operational performance. These insights enable the company to make data-driven decisions that optimize various aspects of its business, from marketing strategies and product development to inventory management and customer service. The ability to quickly and accurately analyze data reduces the time and resources required for decision-making processes, further contributing to cost savings and operational efficiency.

Looking ahead, the future of AI in e-commerce is poised to bring even more transformative changes, with Amazon leading the charge. As AI technology continues to evolve, the next steps in AI-driven retail will likely focus on further personalization, enhanced automation, and the integration of emerging technologies such as augmented reality (AR) and virtual reality (VR). Amazon is well-positioned to spearhead these innovations, leveraging its extensive resources, vast data sets, and commitment to technological advancement.

One of the anticipated trends in AI-driven retail is the rise of hyper-personalized shopping experiences. Building on the success of existing recommendation systems, future AI models will delve deeper into individual customer preferences, lifestyle choices, and even emotional states to provide an unprecedented level of personalization. Amazon's ongoing investment in AI research and development ensures that it remains at the forefront of creating these highly tailored experiences, fostering stronger customer loyalty and driving higher conversion rates.

Enhanced automation will also play a pivotal role in the future of e-commerce. Beyond the current applications in logistics and warehouse operations, AI will increasingly automate complex tasks such as inventory replenishment, dynamic pricing, and real-time fraud detection. Amazon's continuous advancements in AI technology will enable it to implement these sophisticated automation solutions seamlessly, further reducing operational costs and improving overall efficiency.

Moreover, the integration of AR and VR with AI will redefine the way customers interact with products online. Imagine virtually trying on clothes, visualizing how furniture fits into your living space, or experiencing interactive product demonstrations—all facilitated by AI-driven AR and VR technologies. Amazon's exploration of these immersive technologies promises to create more engaging and interactive shopping experiences, bridging the gap between online and offline retail and setting new standards for customer engagement.

Amazon's leadership in AI-driven innovations also extends to sustainability and ethical considerations. As the company continues to develop more efficient and eco-friendly AI solutions, it addresses growing concerns around environmental impact and ethical AI usage. By prioritizing sustainable practices and responsible AI development, Amazon not only enhances its brand reputation but also ensures long-term viability and trust among consumers and stakeholders.

In conclusion, Amazon's strategic integration of artificial intelligence has yielded substantial operational efficiencies and cost savings, reinforcing its position as a leader in the e-commerce and technology sectors. The financial impact of AI on Amazon's operations is evident in reduced costs, optimized logistics, and enhanced productivity, all of which contribute to improved profitability and competitive advantage. Looking to the future, Amazon's commitment to advancing AI-driven innovations promises to further transform the landscape of e-commerce, offering more personalized, efficient, and engaging shopping experiences. As Amazon continues to lead in AI technology, it sets the stage for a new era of retail that is more intelligent, responsive, and customer-centric, ensuring sustained growth and market dominance in the years to come.

Chapter 10: Challenges and Opportunities Ahead

Amazon's ambitious journey into the realm of artificial intelligence is marked by both remarkable achievements and significant challenges. As the company continues to integrate AI into its vast array of services and operations, it encounters a landscape filled with potential obstacles that could impede its progress. Navigating these challenges requires strategic foresight, adaptability, and a commitment to innovation that has long been the hallmark of Amazon's success.

One of the primary obstacles Amazon faces in its AI journey is the complexity of integrating advanced technologies into an already expansive and multifaceted infrastructure. Managing and synchronizing AI systems across diverse sectors such as e-commerce, cloud computing, logistics, and entertainment demands a level of coordination and expertise that is both intricate and resource-intensive. The sheer scale of Amazon's operations means that any disruption or inefficiency in one area can have cascading effects on the entire ecosystem. Additionally, the rapid pace of AI advancements poses a continuous challenge, as the company must stay ahead of emerging technologies and evolving industry standards to maintain its competitive edge.

Another significant challenge lies in ensuring the ethical and responsible deployment of AI technologies. As Amazon develops more sophisticated AI models and integrates them into critical aspects of its business, concerns around data privacy, security, and algorithmic bias become increasingly pertinent. The company must navigate the delicate balance between leveraging vast amounts of data to enhance its AI capabilities and safeguarding the privacy and trust of its customers. Addressing these ethical considerations is not only a moral imperative but also essential for maintaining customer loyalty and regulatory compliance in a world where data protection laws are becoming more stringent.

Moreover, the competition in the AI space is intense, with numerous tech giants and innovative startups vying for dominance. Companies like Google, Microsoft, and Nvidia are continuously pushing the boundaries of AI technology, investing heavily in research and development to create more powerful and efficient models. In this highly competitive environment, Amazon must differentiate its AI offerings and demonstrate clear value propositions to attract and retain customers. The pressure to innovate rapidly while maintaining high standards of quality and reliability adds another layer of complexity to Amazon's AI endeavors.

To overcome these challenges, Amazon employs a multifaceted strategy that leverages its strengths and addresses potential vulnerabilities head-on. Central to this strategy is the company's commitment to continuous innovation and investment in research and development. By dedicating substantial resources to AI research, Amazon ensures that it remains at the forefront of technological advancements, capable of developing cutting-edge solutions that meet the evolving needs of its customers and partners.

Collaboration and strategic partnerships also play a crucial role in Amazon's approach to overcoming obstacles. The deepening of ties with Anthropic, for instance, exemplifies how Amazon leverages external expertise to enhance its AI capabilities. By partnering with leading AI research firms, Amazon gains access to specialized knowledge and innovative technologies that complement its own initiatives. These collaborations foster an environment of shared learning and mutual growth, enabling Amazon to tackle complex AI challenges more effectively and accelerate the development of advanced solutions.

Furthermore, Amazon places a strong emphasis on ethical AI practices, implementing robust frameworks to ensure that its AI technologies are developed and deployed responsibly. This involves rigorous testing for biases, ensuring transparency in AI decision-making processes, and prioritizing data security measures to protect customer information. By proactively addressing these ethical concerns, Amazon builds trust with its customers and stakeholders, reinforcing its reputation as a responsible and forward-thinking technology leader.

In addition to addressing challenges, Amazon is poised to seize numerous opportunities for growth and expansion in the AI landscape. The emergence of new markets and technologies presents avenues for Amazon to extend its AI capabilities and explore innovative business ventures. Areas such as healthcare, finance, and smart home technologies are ripe for AI-driven transformation, offering Amazon the potential to introduce novel solutions that enhance efficiency and improve outcomes in these sectors.

Emerging technologies like augmented reality (AR) and virtual reality (VR) also offer exciting possibilities for integrating AI into more immersive and interactive experiences. By combining AI with AR and VR, Amazon can create sophisticated tools that revolutionize how customers interact with products, visualize their purchases, and engage with digital content. These advancements not only enhance the customer experience but also open up new revenue streams and market opportunities for Amazon.

Moreover, the continued expansion of AI-driven automation presents significant growth prospects for Amazon. As AI technologies become more sophisticated, the potential for automating complex tasks and processes increases, allowing Amazon to further streamline its operations and reduce costs. This enhanced efficiency can translate into more competitive pricing for customers, greater profitability for the company, and the ability to reinvest savings into further innovation and development.

Leveraging AI for new business ventures is another key area where Amazon is set to make substantial strides. By harnessing the power of AI, Amazon can explore and enter new markets with confidence, offering tailored solutions that address specific needs and challenges. Whether it's developing advanced analytics tools for businesses, creating intelligent consumer products, or offering specialized AI services through AWS, Amazon's versatile AI infrastructure provides a solid foundation for launching and scaling new ventures.

The company's foresight in identifying and capitalizing on these opportunities underscores its strategic vision and resilience in the face of an ever-evolving technological landscape. By continuously adapting to new trends and leveraging its AI expertise, Amazon ensures that it remains a leader in innovation, driving growth and maintaining its competitive advantage in the global market.

In conclusion, Amazon's journey through the AI landscape is characterized by both significant challenges and immense opportunities. The company's ability to navigate potential obstacles through strategic innovation, ethical practices, and collaborative partnerships is a testament to its enduring commitment to excellence and leadership in artificial intelligence. As Amazon continues to expand its AI capabilities and explore new avenues for growth, it is well-positioned to lead the next wave of technological advancements, shaping the future of e-commerce, cloud computing, and beyond. The long-term benefits of these efforts extend not only to Amazon and its customers but also to the broader technology ecosystem, fostering a more intelligent, efficient, and interconnected world.

Chapter 11: Ethical Considerations and Responsible AI

As Amazon continues to expand its influence in the realm of artificial intelligence, the company remains acutely aware of the ethical responsibilities that come with such technological advancements. Ensuring that AI systems operate fairly and without inherent biases is paramount, not only for maintaining customer trust but also for upholding the integrity of the services Amazon provides. To address biases and promote fairness in its AI models, Amazon employs rigorous testing and validation processes. These processes involve scrutinizing data sets for any skewed representations and implementing algorithms designed to minimize discriminatory outcomes. By continuously monitoring and refining these models, Amazon strives to create AI systems that treat all users equitably, regardless of their background or personal characteristics.

Amazon's commitment to responsible AI usage extends beyond mere technical adjustments. The company has established comprehensive frameworks that guide the ethical development and deployment of its AI technologies. These frameworks emphasize transparency, accountability, and inclusivity, ensuring that AI applications are designed with a clear understanding of their potential societal impacts. By fostering an environment where ethical considerations are integral to the innovation process, Amazon ensures that its AI initiatives contribute positively to both its business objectives and the broader community. This holistic approach not only mitigates the risks associated with AI but also enhances the overall quality and reliability of the company's technological solutions.

Protecting customer data is another critical aspect of Amazon's ethical AI strategy. In an age where data breaches and privacy concerns are increasingly prevalent, Amazon prioritizes the safeguarding of sensitive information used in AI applications. The company implements robust security measures to protect data from unauthorized access and ensures that data handling practices comply with global privacy regulations. By employing advanced encryption techniques and maintaining stringent access controls, Amazon minimizes the risk of data misuse and reinforces the trust customers place in its platforms. This dedication to data security is essential for maintaining the confidentiality and integrity of customer information, which is foundational to Amazon's reputation and success.

Balancing innovation with privacy concerns is a delicate task that Amazon navigates with careful consideration. While the pursuit of cutting-edge AI technologies drives the company's growth and competitive advantage, it also necessitates a mindful approach to how data is collected, processed, and utilized. Amazon adopts a principle of data minimization, ensuring that only the necessary data is gathered for specific AI functions and that it is used solely for its intended purposes. This approach not only reduces the potential for privacy infringements but also aligns with the growing consumer demand for greater control over personal information. By integrating privacy-by-design principles into its AI development processes, Amazon ensures that innovation does not come at the expense of customer privacy, creating a harmonious balance between technological progress and ethical responsibility.

In essence, Amazon's approach to ethical AI deployment is multifaceted, encompassing efforts to eliminate biases, uphold fairness, protect customer data, and balance innovation with privacy. Through these initiatives, Amazon demonstrates a steadfast commitment to responsible AI usage, ensuring that its technological advancements benefit both the company and its customers in a fair and secure manner. This dedication not only fosters a positive relationship with users but also sets a benchmark for ethical practices within the rapidly evolving landscape of artificial intelligence.

Conclusion

Amazon's journey into artificial intelligence has been nothing short of transformative, marking a pivotal shift in how one of the world's most influential companies operates and innovates. From the inception of Amazon Nova, a comprehensive suite of AI models designed to rival and surpass existing technologies, to the development of proprietary hardware like the Tranium chips and the Ultra Cluster Supercomputer, Amazon has consistently demonstrated its commitment to leading the AI revolution. This strategic pivot has not only enhanced operational efficiency and customer satisfaction but has also positioned Amazon as a formidable competitor in the rapidly evolving AI landscape.

Throughout this exploration, several key themes have emerged, illustrating the depth and breadth of Amazon's AI initiatives. The launch of Amazon Nova, with its diverse range of models tailored to specific applications, showcases Amazon's ability to create versatile and scalable AI solutions that meet the varied needs of its vast ecosystem. The partnership with Anthropic exemplifies how strategic collaborations can amplify technological advancements, fostering an environment of shared innovation and expertise. By integrating AI across every facet of its operations—from customer service and logistics to seller empowerment and content creation—Amazon has seamlessly woven artificial intelligence into the very fabric of its business, driving both efficiency and enhanced user experiences.

The competitive dynamics between Amazon and established players like Nvidia further highlight Amazon's strategic ingenuity. By developing its own AI hardware and challenging Nvidia's dominance in the GPU market, Amazon is not only diversifying its technological assets but also fostering a more competitive and dynamic AI hardware ecosystem. This move underscores Amazon's foresight in recognizing the critical role of specialized hardware in advancing AI capabilities, ensuring that the company remains at the forefront of technological innovation.

Operational efficiency and cost savings have been significant beneficiaries of Amazon's AI integration. Advanced AI models have optimized inventory management, logistics, and warehouse operations, resulting in substantial cost reductions and improved service delivery. These efficiencies translate directly into enhanced customer satisfaction, as products are delivered faster and more reliably, and customer service interactions become more personalized and effective. Case studies throughout this journey have demonstrated the tangible impacts of AI on Amazon's operations, highlighting how strategic AI implementations can drive both financial performance and customer loyalty.

Looking ahead, the future of Amazon and artificial intelligence is poised for even greater advancements. Emerging technologies such as augmented reality and virtual reality, when combined with AI, promise to revolutionize the shopping experience, making it more immersive and interactive. Amazon's ongoing investments in AI research and development, coupled with its strategic partnerships and proprietary innovations, position the company to lead the next wave of AI-driven retail transformations. The potential for hyper-personalized shopping experiences, enhanced automation, and innovative business ventures ensures that Amazon will continue to shape the future of e-commerce and beyond.

The enduring impact of Amazon's AI strategies on the tech landscape cannot be overstated. By prioritizing ethical AI deployment, addressing biases, and safeguarding customer data, Amazon sets a high standard for responsible AI usage. This commitment not only fosters trust and loyalty among customers but also serves as a benchmark for other companies striving to integrate AI into their operations ethically and effectively. Amazon's holistic approach to AI—encompassing software, hardware, partnerships, and ethical considerations—illustrates a comprehensive strategy that other tech giants can look to as a model for sustainable and impactful AI integration.

In conclusion, Amazon's strategic foray into artificial intelligence has redefined its operational capabilities, enhanced customer experiences, and established it as a leader in the AI domain. The company's ability to innovate continuously, navigate complex challenges, and seize emerging opportunities ensures that it remains at the cutting edge of technology. As artificial intelligence continues to evolve, Amazon's unwavering commitment to leveraging AI for growth, efficiency, and customer satisfaction will undoubtedly leave a lasting imprint on the tech landscape, driving forward a future where intelligent systems and human ingenuity coexist to create unprecedented value and progress.

www.ingramcontent.com/pod-product-compliance
Lightning Source LLC
Chambersburg PA
CBHW071032240526
45469CB00006BD/2186